FICTION WRITING WORKBOOK

BY K.L. GLANVILLE

FICTION WRITING WORKBOOK
by K.L. Glanville

Published by Luminations Media Group Inc, Monterey Park, CA
www.LuminationsMediaGroup.com
Printed in the United States of America

Cover by Jeff Milam www.MilamDesigns.com

Audience: Ages 11 to adult

ISBN-13: 978-1-61222-008-6
ISBN-10: 1-612220-08-8

LUMINATIONS
MEDIA GROUP INC.
Monterey Park, California

You Can Write a Story!

This workbook is intended to help YOU become a better fiction writer. The exercises and prompts are for you to practice what you learn as you go. Even if you don't plan on writing a novel just yet, you can learn many writing skills from the exercises. Some of the exercises are related to my book, *The Realm: the Awakening Begins*. Though it's not necessary to read it first, the exercises will be easier to do if you have.

I hope you enjoy making your way through this workbook, creating a world of your own. Let your imagination soar and your dreams wander! Enjoy.

THANK YOU!

Kathy Tyers, Cora Alley & Suzanne Thomas
whose instructive words and "red pens"
helped me to learn a lot of what is in this book

TABLE OF CONTENTS

STORY ARC

STORY ARC

Definition: "the principal plot of an ongoing storyline in the episodes of a narrative; the continuous progression or line of development in a story"[1]

In other words, the story arc is the plot of the story. For every story, you need a story arc. Without a story arc you are simply describing a rambling series of unrelated events. The events may be interesting, but without a story arc, there is no direction. The main character has nothing to be, accomplish, do, or become.

STORY INTRODUCTION:

Have you ever noticed that within about the first five minutes of almost every movie or TV show, or the first few pages of a novel, you are introduced to the following?

- The **main character**(s)
- The **setting** of the story (time & location)
- The **main problem or conflict** needing to be solved or overcome

After the first few pages or minutes, you can have a pretty good idea of what the story will be about.

Let's look closer at each of these parts:

Main Character

The story needs to be about someone, something or someplace. Yes, I did write something or someplace. The main character could be a person, animal, town or even a bush. A town or a bush might be more of a challenge, but I'm sure it can be done with some creativity.

Write down the main characters from your favorite book and movie:

Favorite book main character: _____

Favorite movie main character: _____

---

[1] "story arc." *Dictionary.com's 21st Century Lexicon*. Dictionary.com, LLC. 13 Nov. 2009.
<Dictionary.com http://dictionary.reference.com/browse/story arc>.

Setting

Your story needs to happen somewhere in time and space (or outside of them). You get to choose. Is it in the past, present, future or even outside of time? Is it somewhere in the world we know? California, India, a forest, a messy bedroom, the North Pole? Or is it in outer space? Or maybe it's in a place like heaven, or an imaginary world, or even another dimension! It could involve more than one of these also. It's all up to you! Isn't that great?

What is the setting (time and location) of your favorite story?

_____

_____

_____

Problem/Conflict

As mentioned above, the main character needs something to be, accomplish, do, or become. The main character needs to overcome something. It can be either internal or external, or both.

An **internal problem** means the character has something *inside* them that keeps them from accomplishing a goal.
> Examples:
> - The main character doesn't know how to make friends
> - The main character can't stop lying
> - The main character is afraid of showing love for someone
> - The main character is jealous of his or her friends
> - The main character is afraid to fly

An **external problem** means the character has conflict with someone else, or something they need to overcome *outside* of themselves in order to accomplish a goal.
> Examples:
> - The main character must slay the dragon to save the village
> - The main character must prove she is innocent of the crime
> - The main character must finish building an invention before the mad scientist takes over the world
> - The main character must motivate others to give money so an orphanage can be built
> - The main character must save enough money to buy a new fishing pole to try and win the fishing contest

A **problem that is both internal and external** combines the two types of problems, and both problems must be overcome to reach the goal

>   Examples:
>   - The main character must overcome a fear of failure in order to slay the dragon and save the village
>   - The main character must overcome a dislike of someone so they can work together to build an orphanage
>   - The main character must overcome a fear of flying in order to ride a winged horse to a distant land and gather healing herbs for his or her dying father

What is the problem(s) of the favorite story you wrote about above? Is the problem(s) internal, external or both?

_____

_____

_____

_____

_____

_____

_____

_____

YOU TRY IT

FIND IT IN *THE REALM*:

Who are the main characters? There are actually two in this story:

   1. _____

   2. _____

Re-read pages 1 & 2. What is the setting? There are two settings as well:

_____

_____

_____

What is Graisia's main external problem or conflict, which is set up in these first two pages? See if you can also find another external as well as an internal problem Graisia has.

_____

_____

_____

_____

Look at page 47 and see if you can figure out what Adan's main problem is.

_____

_____

_____

(answers on page 59)

MIDDLE SECTION: TRIALS & ATTEMPTS TO SOLVE THE PROBLEM(S)

Now that the characters, setting, and problem have been introduced, we move on to the whole middle section of the story, where the characters encounter trials related to the problem(s) and try to solve the problem(s).

The picture below shows the possible story arc, or plot of the story. The middle section is full of trials encountered and attempts made. The main character is often trying to run away from the problem – or solve it. Each of these trials or attempts tries to address or solve the problem(s) in some way, but never quite does it. Sometimes it even makes the problem(s) worse!

RESOLUTION

Usually, the problem(s) reaches its climax, or gets its worst, just before there is a final resolution. Resolutions do not all have to be happy. If the resolution is sad, it becomes a tragedy. Either way, the problem(s) is solved.

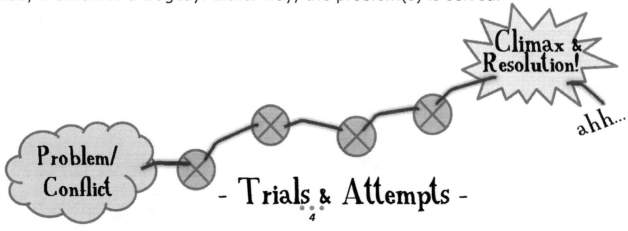

Climax &
Resolution!

ahh...

Problem/
Conflict

- Trials & Attempts -

EXAMPLES FROM *THE REALM*:

WARNING: SPOILER ALERT (If you haven't finished reading the book, you will find out about the ending in this section)

Graisia encounters trouble and attempts on her life from Adan over and over again throughout the book. Each time, she escapes, but Adan is still trying to get her. She cannot seem to get rid of him completely.

Adan also continually tries to hold onto his family's power, even as he goes through many difficult times. Each attempt he makes does not seem to solve his problem. The situation escalates, getting only worse and worse. He tries to keep his power by aligning with Mahalan, holding a séance to try and talk to his dead father, kidnapping Graisia, and ultimately, trying to sacrifice Graisia. However, none of these attempts help him get the power he is looking for.

The **climax** and **resolution** of the story come right before the end of the book. The situations for both Adan and Graisia are at their worst. Graisia is tied up on an altar about to be killed by Adan. Adan is under pressure from Yantir, Handro,[2] Mahalan and even Soliel. His last attempt at gaining enough power is to sacrifice Graisia to Mahalan.

The **resolution** comes as Graisia is miraculously rescued and Adan finally finds a power greater than he has even known. Both of them are now free of the problems introduced at the very beginning of the story.

YOU TRY IT

Think of 1 or 2 main characters you want to write about and describe them briefly

_____

_____

_____

_____

_____

_____

_____

_____

_____

_____

___

[2] For the first printing of The Awakening Begins, "Handro" was spelled "Jandro." We changed this for future printings so readers wouldn't confuse Jandro and Jarón. Jandro and Handro are pronounced the same, and are the same man.

Describe the setting for your story (time, location, etc)

_____

_____

_____

_____

Will the problem be (check one):
☐ Internal
☐ External
☐ Both

Describe the problem(s) for each of your main characters (internal, external or both):

1)_____

_____

_____

_____

_____

_____

2)_____

_____

_____

_____

_____

_____

How will these problems ultimately be resolved in the end of the story? You might not know the complete answer yet, but write as much as you can.

1)_____

_____

_____

_____

2)

THEMES

THEME

Definition: A moral, lesson or idea that is woven throughout a story.

Even if an author writes a story for seemingly no other reason than to entertain, there will most likely be some sort of theme or idea running through the story. Often, it is related to the problem or conflict of the main character(s).

Frequently, there is more than one theme threading its way throughout a story. There can be one main theme and many other **subthemes**.

Sometimes an author may write a book specifically to convey a lesson or idea. It could be a lesson about the need to take care of the environment, love your neighbor, stay in school and out of gangs, be yourself, or any other of myriad themes.

Example from *The Realm*:
There are a number of themes that weave their way through *The Awakening Begins.* One of the main ones is how the power of love is greater than any other kind of power.

YOU TRY IT

FIND IT IN *THE REALM*:
Can you think of any other themes or subthemes in *The Awakening Begins*?

_____

_____

_____

_____

_____

_____

_____

_____

(possible answers on page 59)

In the story arc you wrote about in the previous section, is there a theme that runs through it? If yes, what is it? If no, what theme could run through it? List more than one if you can think of some subthemes you'd like to include.

_____

_____

_____

_____

_____

_____

_____

_____

_____

_____

_____

_____

_____

_____

_____

_____

_____

_____

More on Characters

BACKSTORY

Definition: "a narrative providing a history or background context, esp. for a character or situation in a literary work, film, or dramatic series."[3]

You have to get inside your character's heads and hearts and figure out what makes them tick! This will help your story move along easier.

Each character needs a history that helps explain his or her actions. You may never even write about his or her history in the actual story. But you as the author need to know every main character's history.

Example:

In writing book 2 of *The Realm* Series, I expanded the role of Prime Minister Vivi Sel Luan. I hadn't given her much of a personality in book 1. As I was writing book 2 and putting her in various circumstances, I realized I didn't know how she should respond. So I stopped writing the story and spent some time making up Vivi's backstory. I had to create her history so I could understand why she wanted certain things and why she would act in certain ways. Now, when I put her in a situation, how she should respond becomes almost obvious! The character determines what happens and helps create the story!

When creating a backstory, you can start by thinking first of the end results you want in the character and working your way backwards. Or you can think of the history first and how that would shape him or her in the future. I usually end up doing a combination of the two until I'm happy with the way the character has turned out.

You may find as you are writing that the person's backstory you came up with pops into the actual story now and then to help your reader better understand the character too. That's fine, and it makes for interesting reading.

---

[3] "backstory." *Dictionary.com Unabridged*. Random House, Inc. 13 Nov. 2009.

<Dictionary.com http://dictionary.reference.com/browse/backstory>.

Examples:

In book 1, **Mitina** is a happy-go-lucky little girl. She is full of optimism and kindness. This might not make much sense if she grew up in the slum. But she hasn't lived very long in the slum. She previously lived in the countryside. Until recently, she didn't have to work. Instead she stayed home with her mother and brother. Her personality and reactions to situations make sense because of her history.

Kaly, on the other hand, was basically abandoned by her mother, experienced some rough times in the city and is now just one of many children at her aunt's home. She has had to fend for herself most of her life and struggled with feeling like no one really cares for her, except maybe her *bandhu*. This history and insight helps to explain why she is pretty rough around the edges – and why Graisia's betrayal hurts her so much.

If I hadn't created their histories, I would have had a harder time trying to understand their personalities and knowing how they should respond in various situations.

YOU TRY IT

FIND IT IN *THE REALM*:

Salim is not a main character in most of the books, but he still needs a backstory. In fact, if I ever finish writing a prequel I've started, you will find out that his backstory is huge and it plays a large role in who he is in the other books.

From book 1, what parts of Salim's history do you think explain why he is so afraid to try and bring positive changes to Sawtong?

_____

_____

_____

_____

Knowing some of Graisia's history, why do you think Graisia is not as rough around the edges or as cruel as Kaly?

_____

_____

_____

_____

(answers on page 59-60)

For your story:

Write up a backstory for each of your main characters. Keep in mind the problem(s) they have to overcome or solve in your story. What has given them the internal problem that they have? Why are they afraid, shy, etc.? Why are they the best person to solve the external problem... or maybe the least likely to solve the problem? Why do they want to, or have to, solve it? How did they get into the problem that needs to be fixed in the first place?

NAMES

Sometimes, when I don't feel like writing but I want to do something on the story, I'll spend some time working on the names. It can be lots of fun!

This may seem like an easy topic. But I assure you, there is more to it than meets the eye. Here are a few helpful tips on naming your characters.

Vary the letters that the names start with. If all your names start with the letter "S" it could be hard for the reader to remember who is who. Help the reader by spreading the first letters of the names through the alphabet.

Check on a search engine like Google to see how else the name is used. I found out a little late that the name Opana, in my book, is also the name of a pain medication! Oops!

You might want to create a pronunciation guide if you're going to use unusual names people won't know how to pronounce. You can put it in the back or front of your story.

Name meaning books and websites are great fun to look through for name ideas and their meanings. Also, language dictionaries can be used for getting interesting sounding words that mean something significant.

YOU TRY IT

What did you name your characters above?

_____

_____

_____

Do you want to change their names after reading and following these tips? If yes, what are you changing them to? And why?

_____

_____

_____

_____

_____

_____

TENSE

TENSE:

Definition: "...it expresses the time at which the action described by the verb takes place. The major tenses are past, present, and future."[4]

Your story will need to be written using one of these tenses for the entire story. Inconsistency makes for a lot of confusion. Pick one tense and stick with it! There are two exceptions however, to when you can change tenses. One would be when writing a prophecy (see **Future** below). And the second would be when writing within quotations (see **Tenses and Quotations** below).

PAST, PRESENT OR FUTURE?

Past: Most fictional writing is done using the past tense. The writer writes the story as if it has already happened in the past.

Example: Mitchell lift<u>ed</u> up a huge musty bag of books and <u>set</u> it down on the window seat. He <u>sat</u> down beside it and carefully pull<u>ed</u> out a book from the top of the sack. It look<u>ed</u> like it hadn't been touch<u>ed</u> for 100 years.

Present: Occasionally, an author will write in the present tense.

Example: Sarah look<u>s</u> into the mirror and see<u>s</u> a pimple beginning to form on the end of her nose. A tear trickle<u>s</u> down her cheek. She worri<u>es</u> people will laugh at her when she goe<u>s</u> to school tomorrow.

Future: Very rarely will an author write in future tense except possibly as a prophecy or something similar.

Example: There <u>will be</u> a great flood at the lake in 33 years. The Johnson family <u>will sell</u> their house by the lake just in time. They <u>will be</u> happy and safe in another city when the flood comes.

---

[4] "tense." *The American Heritage® New Dictionary of Cultural Literacy, Third Edition.* Houghton Mifflin Company, 2005. 14 Sep. 2010. <Dictionary.com http://dictionary.reference.com/browse/tense>.

Tenses and Quotations

When writing within quotations, use whichever tense is appropriate to what is being said inside the quotations. In the examples below, note where different tenses are or are not used in the <u>descriptions</u> vs. **quotations**.

Past *(with present in quotes)*: Julie walk<u>ed</u> up the steps and open<u>ed</u> the door. She drop<u>ped</u> her books on the hall table and call<u>ed</u> out to her mother, "**Is** dinner ready?"

Present *(with future in quotes)*: Sam walk<u>s</u> into the house and drop<u>s</u> his backpack on the floor. "What **will we have** for dinner?" he ask<u>s</u>.

Future *(with present and future in quotes)*: The children <u>will arrive</u> home at the same time. They <u>will leave</u> their school books at the door and <u>ask</u> either "**Is** dinner ready?" or "What **will we have** for dinner."[5]

YOU TRY IT

Pick one idea to write about and then write a paragraph about it in each of the three tenses. After you write each paragraph, review it to make sure all the verbs in that paragraph "agree" with each other (they're all the same tense), except for what is in quotations.

Past:

_____

_____

_____

_____

_____

_____

_____

_____

_____

Present:

_____

_____

_____

---

[5] http://en.wikipedia.org/wiki/Narrative_mode#Narrative_point_of_view
Accessed 12:00pm, December 22, 2009

Future:

POV (POINT OF VIEW)

POV (Point of View):

Definition:

"...the vantage point from which a story is presented."[6]

When you write a story, you are always writing from someone's perspective. Two of the more common perspectives are either the POV of one of the characters recounting their story (first-person), or from the viewpoint of a narrator telling the story of others (third-person). Hopefully the definitions and examples below will help you decide how YOU would like to write.

FIRST-PERSON

This is when the author writes as if the story happened to them. For the reader, it's like listening to one of the characters tell the story.

> **Example:** It was a foggy night when I set out to find my cat, Mo. My neighbor's dog, Brutus, had scared him off earlier that evening. I thought Mo would come back, but he hadn't come in for dinner. So I set out with flashlight in hand, down the foggy road toward the wharf.

SECOND-PERSON

Second-person speaks directly to the readers as if they were a character in the story. This is not used very often for writing fiction. It is more often found in poetry and song lyrics. Sometimes it is blended with first person, showing the storyteller's feelings, as in the second example below.

> **Example 1:** You were terrified by that crazy dog, Brutus, and ran top speed down the road toward the wharf, disappearing into the fog. You looked for the closest hiding place you could find. There were no empty boxes or crates on the wharf like there usually were, so you kept running to the end of the wharf. The only place left to hide was on the little boat barely visible through the murky fog. With a brave leap, you jumped the distance and landed on the little skiff.

---

[6] "point of view." © *Encyclopedia Britannica, Inc.*. Encyclopedia Britannica, Inc.. 23 Sep. 2010. <Dictionary.com http://dictionary.reference.com/browse/point of view>.

Example 2 (blended): You ran away from home and I am terribly worried about you, Mo. Don't you know how much it worries me when you don't show up for dinner? Now I must go out in the cold and fog to find you. And who knows? Maybe I'll disappear as well...

THIRD-PERSON

Third-person is used to describe others using "he," "she," "it" and "they". So the storyteller or narrator <u>does not</u> refer to him or herself using "I" or to the reader using "you." Third-person is the most common POV used in fiction writing.

Within the third-person POV, however, there are MANY variations. Four of them are shown in the grid below and are based on the following definitions:

Subjective: Being aware of the feelings held by one or multiple characters
Objective: Not being aware of the feelings of any characters. The narrator only tells what they can "see."
Omniscient: The narrator is given the God-like ability to know everything that is going on in the world of the story.
Limited: The narrator does not know everything that is going on and is limited to only what is in the scene, usually from just one person's perspective.

Combining these definitions together we get the following possibilities:

	Limited	Omniscient
Subjective	<u>**Subjective/Limited**</u> - narrator knows the **feelings & thoughts** of **one** character	<u>**Subjective/Omniscient**</u> - narrator knows **everyone's feelings & thoughts, everywhere**
Objective	<u>**Objective/Limited**</u> - narrator is aware of only what can be **seen** by that <u>one character</u>	<u>**Objective/Omniscient**</u> - narrator knows **everything going on everywhere,** but not thoughts & feelings

So let's explore those possibilities.

Third-Person – Subjective/Limited: The narrator knows the feelings & thoughts of one character.

    Example: Louise was quite worried about her young cat, Mo. When the neighbor's dog had barked at Mo quite loudly that afternoon, he had taken off running down the road. Louise thought he would return for dinner... but dinner time had come and gone. *Where did that poor kitty go?* Louise wondered and worried to herself. She couldn't decide if she should go out looking for him. Would it do any good?

Third-Person – Subjective/Omniscient: The narrator knows everyone's feelings and thoughts, everywhere.

> **Example:** Louise paced the kitchen floor wondering if she should go out into the foggy night to look for her cat. It wasn't like Mo to miss his dinner. *I wish my neighbor would keep better control of her dog,* she thought to herself, *then this wouldn't have happened.*
>
> > Little did she know, her neighbor, Sandy, was out at the pet store looking for a leash for her dog. Sandy felt terrible Brutus had chased her neighbors little cat down the road. If only she'd replaced his broken leash yesterday!

Third-Person – Objective/Limited: The narrator is aware of only what can be seen by the one character

> **Example:** After pacing for a few more moments, Louise grabbed her jacket and flashlight and headed out the door into the cool and misty fog. She walked straight toward the wharf. Her feet clomped on the old wooden boards. Water lapped at the rough round pillars holding the boards above the ocean.
>
> "Mo!" she called out over and over again.

Third-Person – Objective/Omniscient: The narrator knows everything that is going on everywhere, but not thoughts & feelings

> **Example:** Mo mewed softly from inside the boat moored at the end of the wharf.
>
> The fog was so thick. Louise got down on her hands and knees and felt for the edges of the wharf. The flashlight was practically useless. She kept calling Mo, who mewed in return.
>
> She couldn't see him, but Mo had come out of his hiding place inside the boat and was standing on the very front edge of the bow of the boat.
>
> Louise reached the end of the wharf but did not feel Mo anywhere. His mewing was coming from *beyond* the edge of the wharf. Her fingers stumbled upon the rope

holding a boat to the wharf. She gently pulled the rope until a small boat, captained by little Mo, suddenly came into view. Mo jumped into Louise's waiting arms and purred all the way home to dinner.

The Realm... and Being Creative

Have you figured out which way *The Realm: the Awakening Begins* was written? Yes, it's Third-Person – Subjective/Limited, BUT, the subjective/limited point of view shifts between characters throughout the book. The narrator is writing the story about a character as if they could only see, sense and feel what one character is seeing, sensing and feeling. But in different sections, "who that one character is" changes.

There are many ways to mix and match and be creative. Explore the possibilities! Just make sure it isn't confusing to the reader. Let others read it to see if it makes sense and is enjoyable. But first, before you get too fancy, practice the basic forms below. And don't be afraid to only use the basic forms. They're well used for good reason. [7]

---

[7] http://en.wikipedia.org/wiki/Narrative_mode#Narrative_point_of_view
http://www.learner.org/interactives/literature/read/pov2.html
http://www.dummies.com/how-to/content/understanding-point-of-view-in-literature.html
all accessed 12:00pm December 22, 2009

YOU TRY IT

As the examples were written about one scene from many points of view, it's your turn to try it. Start with a scene you'd like to put in your story, or about something that happened recently to you, or something entirely different. It's up to you. Just make it the same scene throughout the exercises.

First-Person:

_____
_____
_____
_____
_____
_____
_____
_____
_____
_____
_____
_____
_____

Second-Person (simple or blended):

_____
_____
_____
_____
_____
_____
_____
_____
_____
_____
_____
_____
_____
_____
_____

Third-Person – Subjective/Limited:

_____
_____
_____
_____
_____
_____
_____
_____
_____
_____
_____
_____
_____

Third-Person – Subjective/Omniscient:

_____
_____
_____
_____
_____
_____
_____
_____
_____
_____
_____
_____
_____

Third-Person – Objective/Limited:

_____
_____
_____
_____
_____
_____
_____

Third-Person – Objective/Omniscient:

After writing each of these, which is(are) your favorite?

 # THE SENSES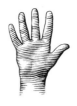

Sometime in Kindergarten, you probably learned about the 5 senses.

Sight * Hearing * Taste * Touch * Smell

What you probably didn't learn in Kindergarten is how important it is to use the senses when writing!

When you write, use sensory descriptions throughout your story. When you write about what your characters are hearing, seeing, feeling, smelling and tasting, it helps the readers to feel like they're immersed in your story.

<u>Caution:</u> Do not get too carried away and try and include all of the senses at once. Use them wisely.

Example: The following paragraph from *The Realm* is packed with descriptions that engage the reader's imagination with sensory descriptions. The sensory description phrases are underlined, followed below by the sense(s) they evoke.

"The <u>warm humid air</u> foretold another sweltering day in the sun. Graisia's torn and <u>grubby dress, two sizes too small, clung to her already sweating body in the heat.</u> Her <u>feet kicked up dust</u> as she headed off, flip-flops <u>flapping awkwardly against her heels, like newly caught fish slapping in a bucket.</u>" (p. 7)

<u>warm humid air:</u> **touch:** warm, wet

<u>grubby dress:</u> **sight:** state of her clothes

<u>two sizes too small:</u> **touch:** it would feel tight

<u>clung to her already sweating body in the heat:</u> **touch:** warmth, wet, discomfort

<u>feet kicked up dust:</u> **touch:** feet feel the soft dust; **taste** or **smell:** if the dust was really getting kicked up she might have to breathe it in her mouth or nose; **sight:** creates an image of dust clouds forming around her feet

<u>flapping awkwardly against her heels, like newly caught fish slapping in a bucket:</u> **hearing:** the flip flops flapped; **touch:** flapping against her skin

YOU TRY IT

FIND IT IN *THE REALM*:

Below is the first paragraph from *The Realm: the Awakening Begins.* <u>Underline</u> each phrase that is a sensory description.

Graisia stared in horror at Adan's eyes. They flickered like flames, reflecting the blood-red, eerie light of the darkened sky. His face hovered so close she could feel his stale, warm breath that seemed full of slithering worms. She wanted to turn and run, but there was no place to go. She stood backed up against the wall of someone's shack of a home, trapped at the dead end of one of the winding dirt paths that snaked through their makeshift town near the dump. Terror raced up and down her spine like needle pricks, and splinters pressed into her back from the rough wood. Her thin, worn dress gave her about as much protection as a flimsy layer of onion skin.

Write the phrases you underlined and tell which sense or senses they use. Some have more than one possible answer.

_____

_____

_____

_____

_____

_____

_____

_____

_____

_____

_____

_____

_____

_____

_____

_____

(answers on page 60)

For your story:

Using the character(s), setting(s) and problem(s) you wrote about earlier, write at least one paragraph that uses  sensory descriptions. Try to get your readers to feel like they are totally in the story by using descriptions that evoke some or all of their senses. And remember, it's probably best NOT to use ALL of the senses in one paragraph.

Note: Some people might consider sensing with one's spirit another sense. Feel free to add sensing something **spiritually** to your "toolbox" of senses.

FORESHADOWING

Definition: Giving hints about major events or story developments earlier in the story.

Foreshadowing is used for at least three reasons:
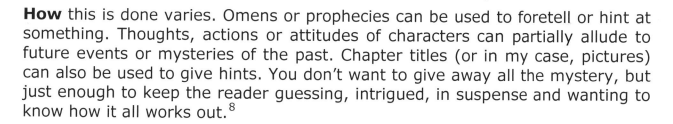
- To drop hints about solutions to mysteries
- To provide consistency throughout a story, so the reader is not unduly startled by something that would seem inconsistent if it was only introduced later in a story or series.
- To hint at the future resolution

How this is done varies. Omens or prophecies can be used to foretell or hint at something. Thoughts, actions or attitudes of characters can partially allude to future events or mysteries of the past. Chapter titles (or in my case, pictures) can also be used to give hints. You don't want to give away all the mystery, but just enough to keep the reader guessing, intrigued, in suspense and wanting to know how it all works out.[8]

Sometimes you might not add the foreshadowing in the first draft. You might not know what needs foreshadowing until you've written a draft or two. Then you can go back and add foreshadowing hints along the way, like breadcrumbs throughout the story.

Or if you're like a friend of mine, you might outline the whole story thoroughly from the beginning so that you know exactly what needs foreshadowing as you go along.

> **Tip:**
> Did you catch that? I said you might write **a draft or two** before adding some of the foreshadowing? I can't even count how many drafts there were of *The Awakening Begins*. I lost count. I was probably still adding foreshadowing at draft thirty! Just because you have to rewrite something doesn't mean you're a failure. You're just making it better. Keep it up!

---

[8] http://www.internetwritingworkshop.org/pwarchive/pw21.shtml accessed 1-1-10, 9pm

Examples from *The Realm*:

In *The Awakening Begins,* I used foreshadowing in a number of places.

- There are prophecies and omens (by Rawiya, Ivah and Opana) given to foretell possible future events. Rawiya's prophecy tells us that Soliel has an important role to play that has to do with the destiny of the town. The legends of Ivah tell of her future importance and connection with Soliel. Opana's reading of Graisia's omen shows that some spiritual force was tuned in to some bad plans in store for Graisia.
- Salim and Estar don't come into the story in a big way until after page 200, yet they're very important characters. Because of this, I had to go back and weave them in a little bit in the beginning. I had Graisia encounter them along the path to introduce them (p. 19). Then soon after, Kaly taunted Graisia about them. I wanted their characters to be imprinted in the reader's mind from the beginning.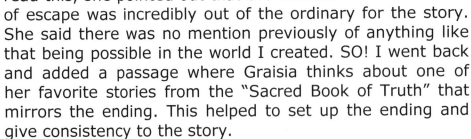
- (Spoiler Alert) In the resolution of T*he Awakening Begins*, Graisia is whisked away by Uri to safety. It's done in such a way that she moves faster than can naturally be done. When one of my editors read this, she pointed out that the method of escape was incredibly out of the ordinary for the story. She said there was no mention previously of anything like that being possible in the world I created. SO! I went back and added a passage where Graisia thinks about one of her favorite stories from the "Sacred Book of Truth" that mirrors the ending. This helped to set up the ending and give consistency to the story.
- The chapter pictures give hints about what might be in the chapter.
- The Prime Minister, Vivi Sel Luan, is not a main character in book 1, but I knew I wanted her to be a more significant character in book 2. For that reason, I made sure to mention her a few times throughout book 1 to prepare readers for the next book. I wanted readers to know she belonged in the series when they started reading book 2.

YOU TRY IT

Go back to your story arc ideas in the first section of this workbook, where you wrote about the resolution(s) of the main character(s) problem(s). For each of the resolutions, list two or three hints you could weave throughout your story and how you might mention them.

_____
_____
_____
_____
_____
_____
_____
_____
_____
_____
_____
_____
_____
_____
_____
_____
_____
_____
_____
_____
_____
_____
_____

DIALOGUE

HE SAID, SHE SAID

You've probably heard it by now: using the word "said" all the time in dialogue is not very interesting. In fact, it actually can be, if used the right way. You *can* use alternatives to said, but most of the time, simple words like "said," "asked" and "replied," work just fine. Too many "said" words, or variations of the word "said," can be distracting. At times, if a line of dialogue really needs to be tagged with how they said it, you can add a line of description after "said." Example: "That's all," she said, climbing off her soapbox.

Another alternative to "said" words is to simply use actions to show what the character was doing when they spoke. This can give insight into the meaning as well as help the readers identify who is speaking.

If the dialogue is clear enough, you might not even tell who is speaking or how they spoke, because the readers can easily figure it out for themselves.

Examples from *The Awakening Begins*.

"I thought you said everyone had light." Graisia **said, turning** to Estar.	> "said" combined with action
"True, everyone gives off light, but there's a brighter light placed deep within a person when they've truly met the king," Estar **replied, tilting her head a little**. "You know, his light is the brightest and purest, and it's in you now. That can upset other beings, and people."	> "replied" combined with action
"The king?" Graisia **asked, surprised and confused**. She'd never met any king.	> "asked" combined with emotions (saying and using HER emotions are okay because we're reading from HER subjective/limited POV)
"Jarón," Estar **stated matter-of-factly**.	> "stated matter-of-factly"
Graisia **was shocked**. "I didn't know he was a king. He didn't tell me that." But she definitely remembered the light coming from Jarón into her – Uri's incredible light!	> telling Graisia's feeling before the quote tells us how she said it
"He's not just *a* king, he's the *High* King, lovey, with many kings and queens under him."	> No "said" words or hints needed, the reader can figure out who said it and how because of the following sentence
(p.218-219)	

8 PUNCTUATION RULES FOR DIALOGUE

1.   **Each character's speaking should be in separate paragraphs.**

"I want to make some cookies," Marilyn told James.
"Great! What kind are you going to make?" James asked. He loved cookies and his favorites were peanut-butter chocolate-chip.

2.   **The quote and the way it is said should be separated by a comma. This is true only if where the comma is, would normally be a period.**

"I thought I'd make some chocolate-chip cookies," Marilyn **answered**.

3.   **The comma is also needed when the quote comes AFTER the way it is said. When this happens, you capitalize the beginning of the quote too.**

Marilyn squealed gleefully**, "They're** my favorite!"

4.   **If the quote ends with a question or exclamation mark, use those punctuation marks instead of a comma.**

"Will you eat some if I make them**?**" Marilyn asked James.

5.   **If the word starting the description phrase *after* a quote is NOT a proper noun, do not capitalize it. This is true even if the quote ends in a question or exclamation mark.**

"Could you add peanut-butter too**?**" **h**e asked back.
"I think you ate the last of the peanut-butter at lunch," **s**he teased.

6.   **If you are not describing how it was *said*, but rather something the character is doing or feeling, the quote and the description become separate sentences. Commas are no longer used to separate them.**

"I did not**.**" James **crossed his arms and pouted playfully**.
Marilyn **shrugged her shoulders** and **smiled.** "You always eat up all the peanut-butter in the house."

7.   If you are interrupting the quote to tell the way something is said, put the comma (or appropriate punctuation) and the lowercase words joined with the part of the quote it describes. Make sure you capitalize the second part if it starts a new sentence.

James looked at the ceiling, deep in thought. "Hey**!**" **he** suddenly exclaimed**.** "**M**aybe we could walk to the store and get some more!"

8.   If the "said" words describe both parts of the quote, put commas on either end of the description. If the "said" words interrupt the quote mid sentence, the second part of the quote will not be capitalized.

Marilyn thought for a moment. "If you have some money**,**" **she said slowly,** "**w**e should have time to do that."

YOU TRY IT

Below is a dialogue that has some punctuation and capitalization errors. Circle the errors and put the corrections above the error. If something just shouldn't be there, x it out.

Remember the punctuation and capitalization differences between quotes set off by actions or feelings vs. quotes set off by "said" words.

Example:
    "I told you, Mom went to the store." The girl stated.

    "Oh yeah," her sister scratched her head, "I forgot."

Your Turn:

Lola and Marcus sat on the front steps of Lola's house.

"What did you do for the summer"? Lola asked.

"Well" Marcus answered "we went to the lake a few times. That was fun." He

threw a pebble across the lawn like he was skipping it on the lake. "how about

your family?"

Lola smiled, "we went to my grandmother's house."

"That doesn't sound too fun." Marcus responded, "why are you smiling?"

"Oh!" "My grandmother is a wonderfully entertaining storyteller, my cousins were there, there's an enormous bookstore nearby, the beach isn't far away, and—"

"Okay, okay! I get the picture"! Marcus laughed

"Yeah, it was pretty good" She said as she leaned back on her elbows. "Are you doing anything for Christmas break?

"Christmas?" he was stunned, "we haven't even started school up again!"

"Well what would you want to do?" she loved to think ahead.

Marcus shook his head and smiled, "I'd rather just enjoy your company right now. There's time to think of Christmas later,"

(answers on page 60-61)

What About Thoughts?

When writing a character's thoughts, different authors vary in style. There is no set rule on how to punctuate thoughts. Some treat them exactly the same as dialogue, others don't use any special punctuation. In *The Realm* series, I used all the same rules as with dialogue EXCEPT I put the words in *italics* and did not use quotation marks.

Example:
Jeremy looked out the window toward his neighbor's house. *I wonder if she'll come home today*, he thought to himself. *She must be really enjoying her vacation. She's been gone for over two weeks!*

KEEPING IT IN PERSPECTIVE!

When using "said" words and writing the surrounding descriptions of the character and their feelings during dialogue, it is VERY important to keep the type of POV you are using in mind.

For instance, if you are writing from **first person** or **third person subjective/limited** (see pages 21-24), you will only be aware of the main person's internal perspective. In other words, you will only be able to directly describe the main character's emotions and thoughts – something that is often done in the descriptions surrounding dialogue.

In *The Realm*, I had to get creative. When I wanted the reader to have at least a hint of what another character was thinking, I gave special attention to the way the person spoke or something they did that gave a hint of their hidden intentions or feelings. Other times I had the character – whose POV I was writing from – guess what the other character was thinking or feeling.

Below is a section from Graisia's POV showing examples of both revealing Graisia's thoughts AND trying to further reveal what Kaly might be thinking and feeling through her actions and expressions. Besides the words from the quotes themselves, **notice** the differences in how thoughts and emotions are revealed for Graisia versus Kaly.

Looking exasperated, Kaly took over the explanation. "Soliel went and made an alliance with Ivah. Now she supposedly has power to heal and help people." **She wrinkled her nose, indicating how foolish she thought this was.** "Adan's not happy about it. He's probably afraid she's going to take over the town."

Graisia glanced back at Pouyan's shack, **concerned** for Salim. Salim stood just inside the doorway, filling their bags with old shoes. "I don't think Adan would want to hurt Salim. He's not trying to take over Sawtong or anything." She turned back to the others, **trying to believe her own argument.**

"Soliel just says she wants to do good," Kaly **warned**, "and it sure isn't keeping her out of trouble. You better be careful going after some other spirit god, whoever this Uri is. I'm sure Salim isn't called crazy for nothing."

Despite a growing fear, Graisia also felt a little happier. Kaly actually **seemed concerned** about her.

As if Kaly realized her feelings had shown, she **hardened her face** again. "But it's up to you if you want to get into more trouble. At least we got our money out of you before you skipped on us."

Graisia swallowed. **Maybe she wasn't totally forgiven**. (p. 232-233)

Whichever POV you use, make sure your descriptions outside of the quotations, match it. Always stay in the POV you've chosen.

YOU TRY IT

Using what you've learned so far and two characters you've created, write one paragraph of dialogue two different ways – from two different types of POV (reference pages 21-24). At this point, don't worry if it will actually fit into a story line – but do stay consistent with their character.

1. Type of POV chosen: _____

_____

_____

_____

_____

_____

_____

_____

_____

_____

_____

_____

_____

_____

_____

_____

_____

_____

_____

_____

_____

_____

On the next page, write the same dialogue as above (use the same words within the quotation marks) but from a different POV.

2. Type of POV chosen: _____

_____

_____

_____

_____

_____

_____

_____

_____

_____

_____

_____

_____

_____

_____

_____

_____

_____

_____

_____

_____

_____

SHOWING VS. TELLING

Below is the dialog I used previously for explaining the dialogue punctuation rules. In most of this dialogue, only simple substitutions for the word "said" were used.

"I want to make some cookies," Marilyn told James.

"Great! What kind are you going to make?" James asked. He loved cookies and his favorites were peanut butter chocolate-chip.

"I thought I'd make some chocolate-chip cookies," Marilyn answered, then squealed gleefully, "They're my favorite!" She then asked James, "Will you eat some if I make them?"

"Could you add peanut butter too?" he asked back.

"I think you ate the last of the peanut butter at lunch," she teased.

"I did not." James crossed his arms and pouted playfully.

Marilyn shrugged her shoulders and smiled. "You always eat up all the peanut butter in the house."

James looked at the ceiling, deep in thought. "Hey!" he suddenly exclaimed. "Maybe we could walk to the store and get some more!"

Marilyn thought for a moment. "If you have some money," she said slowly, "we should have time to do that."

Paint word pictures: Have you ever heard the saying, **"A picture is worth a thousand words?"** It's actually true in writing... sort of. You can use words to paint a picture. The more you describe the picture of what is going on in the scene, the more the reader will understand what is happening. So much more can be added to what is being said in a dialogue when you paint a picture with words surrounding it.

TAKE 2! Below, the dialogue remains the same, but notice the difference it makes to use descriptions of feelings, thoughts and actions instead of only "said" words. It is written in the subjective/omniscient POV.

Marilyn's stomach growled loudly. She looked longingly toward the kitchen then turned to her brother, James. "I want to make some cookies."

"Great! What kind are you going to make?" James ran into the kitchen and started pulling down the flour, sugar, a bowl and a mixing spoon. He opened another cupboard and started looking for the peanut butter. He loved cookies and his favorites were peanut butter, chocolate chip.

"I thought I'd make some chocolate chip cookies," Marilyn answered as she opened up another cupboard and pulled out some chocolate chips. Holding the chocolate chips, she squealed gleefully and spun around the kitchen in a spontaneous pirouette. "They're my favorite!" Then she stopped and looked at James with mock seriousness. "Will you eat some if I make them?"

"Could you add peanut butter too?" he asked as he searched for the peanut butter jar.

"I think you ate the last of the peanut butter at lunch," she teased.

"I did not." James turned around and crossed his arms, pouting playfully.

Marilyn shrugged her shoulders and smiled. "You always eat up all the peanut butter in the house." She walked over to the recycle bin, pulled out the empty peanut butter jar and held it out for him to see.

He pretended not to notice. Instead, he looked up at the ceiling as if deep in thought. "Hey!" he suddenly exclaimed. "Maybe we could walk to the store and get some more!"

Marilyn thought for a moment. She had friends coming over later, and she was really hungry. But she also knew how much her brother loved peanut butter in his cookies. "If you have some money," she said slowly, "we should have time to do that."

James pulled a couple dollars out of his pocket and smiled at her.

Balance: Just as with anything, balance is important. You don't want your actions, feelings and thoughts to distract from the dialogue. You want it to flow naturally. If you have too much description, it gets muddy.

Tip:
When writing dialogue, try reading your dialogue out loud to someone or have someone read it out loud to you. See if it flows naturally as it is read. Sometimes simply hearing your words out loud helps you see places that could use some editing.

YOU TRY IT

Now it's your turn to write your own dialogue. Using the characters and story arc you've already come up with, write a dialogue that could take place somewhere in your story. Make sure you indent each paragraph and have your punctuation and capitals in the right places!

_____

_____

_____

_____

_____

_____

_____

_____

_____

_____

_____

_____

_____

_____

_____

_____

_____

_____

_____

_____

_____

_____

_____

_____

RESEARCH

When you think about fiction, you might not automatically think research would be involved. But depending on your topic, **research can be crucial**.

I wanted *The Realm Series* to have a lot of realistic **supernatural** occurrences in it. So for many years, I read books and talked with people from around the world so I could hear their stories.

I also wanted the series to be set in a realistic type of **slum town**. For this, I also read books and talked with people, and visited various places around the world. In the end, I didn't know one particular place well enough to make it the setting for my book, so I combined a lot of what I knew and made up my own country! After writing the book, I asked friends who had visited or worked in very poor areas to read it and tell me if it sounded authentic. If they had said no, I would have asked them for advice on how to change it.

One thing I did not expect to be told to research was on how to use a **knife**! In *The Awakening Begins*, there is one part where Adan wants to kill someone with a knife. One of my editors read a draft of my book and told me Adan

wasn't using the knife correctly if he wanted to kill someone. I didn't know that. I had never tried to kill someone... and never will! My editor hadn't tried to kill anyone either, but she had researched the topic for one of her books. Now I had to do some research. I had to figure out how Adan would use a knife, because he would know... even if I wouldn't.

For book 2 in the series, part of the story has to do with a **nuclear power plant**. I had no idea how they worked. I wanted something in particular to happen with it in my story. So I went to my cousin who is a nuclear engineer. He was able to tell me what I needed to know and proofread the sections. If any other nuclear engineer ever reads my book, they will know I know what I'm talking about!

YOU TRY IT

Thinking of the story idea you've begun in this workbook, what are two things you might need to research?

1)_____

_____

2)_____

_____

What will your strategy be for researching each of them? Internet? Books? Knowledgeable person? If a knowledgeable person, who?

1)_____

_____

2)_____

_____

Start your research:
Pick one of the things you need to research and follow through with one of your strategies. Write down some of what you find below.

_____

_____

_____

_____

_____

_____

_____

_____

_____

_____

_____

_____

_____

_____

_____

_____

FUN

YES. You are allowed to have fun!

I love to have fun in whatever I'm doing... and that includes writing! Why do you think I included pictures on almost every page in this workbook? It makes it more fun – for both you and me!

Don't be afraid to have fun with writing. In fact, I LOOK for ways to have fun with my writing. I often enjoy creating characters, giving them a backstory, imagining the setting, and writing the actual adventure. Here are some things to do that can make writing even more fun than it already is.

- ❖ Add pictures – you can draw them, hire someone else to draw them, or use royalty free clipart/photos

- ❖ Be creative with names. Choose names with significant meanings

- ❖ Invent place names and/or words used by your characters

- ❖ Create a new world for your characters to live in

- ❖ Write a prologue or introduction that will intrigue the reader (example from *The Awakening Begins*: Ramel's pledge to Mahalan, written on a paper bag).

- ❖ Make sure the end of each chapter is a "cliff hanger" that will make the reader want to keep reading

- ❖ Invent your own language (or part of one)

- ❖ Make a website to advertise your story (one of my favorite places to design websites is at www.WIX.com, and it's free!)

I LOVE to have fun when writing.
If I didn't have fun
I don't think I'd want to write anymore!

IDEA FILE

WRITE IT DOWN:

One thing I learned while writing my book was to **write down ideas when they came**. I never knew when they would come, so I ended up carrying paper and pen/pencil with me at all times... even on a walk or going shopping! Now I use my cell phone to write notes to myself – either way works!

I discovered **if I didn't** write down an idea when it came, I would either forget the idea, or if I got another idea, it would push the first idea out and I could only remember one of them! It didn't take me too long to realize I needed to value each one as they came and WRITE IT DOWN right at that moment.

I wrote notes and vignettes (short scenes) for three years before setting out to actually write the book in chapter form. By the end of those three years, I had a pile of pages of notes I could sift through, sort and organize.

I suggest that you get something like a file folder, envelope, computer, or box where you can keep all of your valuable ideas. If you're getting ideas for more than one story or project, use multiple file folders, etc. I use file folders for some notes and files on my computer for a lot of my ideas. Sometimes I'll write it first on paper or my cell phone and then transfer it to my computer when I get home.

However you do it, value your wonderful, brilliant inspirations when they come. And incidentally... this doesn't just apply to writing. It can apply to ideas for any area of your life. Keep track of them!

YOU TRY IT

How are you going to keep track of your notes and ideas? File folders? Box? Envelope? 3x5 cards? Computer? Write down your plan below.

_____

_____

_____

TYPES OF IDEAS YOU MIGHT WANT TO COLLECT:

- **Character ideas:** When you see or meet someone particularly interesting or with interesting features or characteristics, you could jot down notes about them and file them away under characters. The next time you're trying to think of a type of person for a story, look at your notes!
- **Characters you dream up yourself**
- **Story ideas** that fits someplace in your story other than what you're working on right now.
- **Book ideas:** what you may want to write next
- **Movie ideas**
- **Articles** you might want to write
- **Questions to research**
- **Craft ideas:** things you could make (if you have a digital camera, you can take pictures of things you want to make, print or save them and file them away!)
- **Inventions**
- **Recipe ideas**
- **Music lines for songs**
- **Business ideas:** Do you have dreams of owning your own business someday?
- **Ways to help others:** If you could do something to help others, what would it be? How could you do it?
- **Toys/Games:** Have you ever thought, "Someone should invent a toy/game like…" and you've finished the sentence? Jot it down. Who knows? Maybe someday, you'll be able to make it!

What other kinds of ideas could you write down to keep?

_____

_____

_____

_____

Now, before you do anything else, **follow through on the plan** you wrote above. If you need supplies, figure out how and when you can get them. If you already have what you need, set it up and label it (a file, envelope, box or file on your computer). You can even decorate it if you want. Make it fun and personal.

Remember! If you don't write it down, you just might lose it!

FINAL NOTES & SECRETS

~~EDITERS~~ *Editors*

Have you ever gotten an essay back with tons of red marks on it, and it makes your heart feel like it's sinking to your toes? You feel defeated, not good enough, a failure? Well, it might not be that bad. I used to hate red marks or any kind of corrections on my writing. It made me feel like a failure. I wanted to be perfect. But we all know THAT is impossible. We ARE on a journey, however, to become the best we can be.

So here's a secret. Learn to love those red marks. Don't be afraid of red. Red is good. Red means you have an opportunity to become better.

I remember one of the first times I hired an editor to read *The Awakening Begins*. I got back the manuscript and a cover letter. There were SO many things the editor found wrong with it, he suggested I start all over again! I was so discouraged I don't think I looked at it again for a couple of months.

After the pain and shock wore off a bit, I went paragraph by paragraph, looking at all his suggestions. Some of them I decided to take, and some I did not.

> Something I learned in this process is that getting the opinions of others is good, but you don't have to take all their advice. In the midst of learning from someone else, you need to remain true to the story YOU are trying to convey.

It turned out that the suggestions I DID take from this editor helped to make the book much more suspenseful and exciting. He also helped with ideas on how to make the characters more interesting. But I didn't start all over again.

Then there were all my friends and members of my targeted audience who read it or heard me read it…. They found things wrong with my story too. Or, they had questions. At first, I was bothered by this. I didn't want people to point out my mistakes. But eventually I saw how much their help made the story better.

Now, when I give a manuscript to someone to edit, I think, **"Here, please make my story better!"** Yes, I still get a little nervous anticipating how *many* places they will find for improvement. I have to repeatedly choose to swallow my pride. But I know that the end product will turn out **SO MUCH BETTER.**

PATIENCE

Be patient with yourself. Writing a good story can be a long journey. For my first book, it took eight years to go from idea to holding a published book in my hand. Three years of taking notes and doing research. Five years of writing, refining, writing, refining, drawing pictures, hiring a cover artist, etc. and finally, publishing.

(Don't worry, the following books in the series are coming much quicker...)

PERSISTENCE

In those eight years, I'm sure I had friends that doubted I would EVER finish. Two of the things that helped me along the way were 1) realizing how important and time consuming research is (mentioned earlier) and 2) doing a little bit every day.

If you have a bucket that needs to be filled with water and you put a teaspoon in every day, eventually it will get full... if you don't give up. There were some days all I felt like doing was figuring out a name for a character. So that's what I did. It didn't seem like much, but that was something I wouldn't have to do tomorrow!

Don't look at the whole thing and feel overwhelmed. Find one thing you can do today, whether it's writing a scene or a sentence, naming a chapter or a character, or thinking through a character's history. You've done something!! Be content and proud of yourself for doing something. Eventually... it will get done... when you do SOMETHING each day.

Eventually, you will have...

Your Story!

HEADS UP ON SEQUELS

After you finish your first book, you might be so full of story that you want to write a sequel or two, or three, or more!

When considering writing a sequel, there are a few unique things worth thinking about. When embarking on writing book 2, I discovered a lot of helpful suggestions simply by searching "how to write a sequel," or something similar, on the internet. I would suggest you do the same. You will find far more than I can easily include here. I have, however, included two tips and three links below to get you headed in the right direction.

Foreshadowing

First of all, hopefully, you've been thinking of things you want to put in the sequels while writing book 1. This way, you can add foreshadowing elements as you go. If you didn't, you might want to consider going back and adding in some foreshadowing in the first or earlier books as you plan and work on the following books. Sometimes this is not entirely possible – like when book 1 is already published! But as you write, try and think ahead about some of the main points, characters and story lines in future books you might write.

Bring in the NEW!

Second, the story arc in sequels should not be simply a rehashing of the previous story arc(s). This means the problems the characters face and the solutions they find need to be NEW.

New challenges need to be introduced. You might also want to introduce new characters. Previous characters also need to have developed and grown, facing different issues than they faced in previous books.

Helpful Links:

http://writing-novels.suite101.com/article.cfm/writing_the_sequel_iii_plotlines
http://writing-genre-fiction.suite101.com/article.cfm/writing_the_sequel_i_villains
http://writing-novels.suite101.com/article.cfm/writing_the_sequel_ii_heroes

FIND IT IN *THE REALM*:

If you have read book 2 in *The Realm Series*:

Pick out some elements from book 2 that were foreshadowed in book 1 (*The Awakening Begins*).

_____
_____
_____
_____
_____
_____
_____

(possible answers on page 61)

What were the new problems and solutions for Graisia and Adan in book 2?

_____
_____
_____
_____
_____
_____
_____
_____

(possible answers on page 61)

CHECK LIST

Now that you've learned about the various parts of a story and have notes on your story arc and characters, it's time to write YOURS! Below is a check list to use as you write your story. It does not have to be done in order or all at once.

- ☐ In your first couple of paragraphs/pages
    - ☐ Introduce your main characters
    - ☐ Describe the setting
    - ☐ Introduce the problem or conflict that will need to be resolved
    - ☐ Use a lot of sensory detail in your descriptions
- ☐ Do you have a theme in your story? What is it? _____
  _____
- ☐ Backstory for your main and supporting characters
    - ☐ ☐ Main characters   ☐ ☐ ☐ ☐ Supporting characters
- ☐ Names
    - ☐ With different first letters
    - ☐ Interesting definitions if you choose
    - ☐ "Google" to check possible other uses of name if using unusual names
    - ☐ Pronunciation guide in the back of the story if you want one
- ☐ ☐ ☐ ☐ Trials and attempts at solving the main problem(s)
- ☐ ☐ ☐ Research something you want to write about
- ☐ ☐ Resolution/solution foreshadowed in at least two places
- ☐ Exciting climax and resolution
- ☐ Lots of sensory descriptions throughout the story (without going overboard)
- ☐ In dialogue
    - ☐ Double check for correct punctuation
- ☐ Check to make sure your whole story is written in the same tense (most likely the past tense)
- ☐ Check for consistency in point of view (POV)
- ☐ Make sure to do "fun" things throughout the story (check all that apply to you)
    - ☐ Pictures
    - ☐ Meaningful names
    - ☐ Invent words/language
    - ☐ Write a prologue
    - ☐ Cliffhangers at the end of chapters
    - ☐ Make a website
    - ☐ Other!
- ☐ Editing – have a number of people edit different drafts or sections as you go along and give you feedback. Remember, don't be afraid of the red!
    - ☐ ☐ ☐ Teacher/Editor   ☐ ☐ ☐ Parent or Adult   ☐ ☐ ☐ Peer/friend
    - ☐ ☐ ☐ Members of Target Audience
- ☐ Idea folder started for future projects!

CHECK LIST FOR YOUR SECOND BOOK!

Remember: the list below does not have to be done in order or all at once.
At the bottom are spaces for you to add items you discover that could be related to sequels.

- ☐ In your first couple of paragraphs/pages
    - ☐ Introduce your main characters
    - ☐ Describe the setting
    - ☐ Introduce the problem or conflict that will need to be resolved
    - ☐ Use a lot of sensory detail in your descriptions
- ☐ Do you have a theme in your story? What is it? _____
  _____
- ☐ Backstory for your main and supporting characters
    - ☐ ☐ Main characters   ☐ ☐ ☐ ☐ Supporting characters
- ☐ Names
    - ☐ With different first letters
    - ☐ Interesting definitions if you choose
    - ☐ "Google" to check possible other uses of name if using unusual names
    - ☐ Pronunciation guide in the back of the story if you want one
- ☐ ☐ ☐ ☐ Trials and attempts at solving the main problem(s)
- ☐ ☐ ☐ Research something you want to write about
- ☐ ☐ Resolution/solution foreshadowed in at least two places
- ☐ Exciting climax and resolution
- ☐ Lots of sensory descriptions throughout the story (without going overboard)
- ☐ In dialogue
    - ☐ Double check for correct punctuation
- ☐ Check to make sure your whole story is written in the same tense (most likely the past tense)
- ☐ Check for consistency in point of view (POV)
- ☐ Make sure to do "fun" things throughout the story (check all that apply to you)
    - ☐ Pictures
    - ☐ Meaningful names
    - ☐ Invent words/language
    - ☐ Write a prologue
    - ☐ Cliffhangers at the end of chapters
    - ☐ Make a website
    - ☐ Other!
- ☐ Editing – have a number of people edit different drafts or sections as you go along and give you feedback. Remember, don't be afraid of the red!
    - ☐ ☐ ☐ Teacher/Editor   ☐ ☐ ☐ Parent or Adult   ☐ ☐ ☐ Peer/friend
    - ☐ ☐ ☐ Members of Target Audience
- ☐ Idea folder started for future projects!
- If a sequel: ☐ Foreshadowing in book 1   ☐ New Story Arc (problems/solutions)
- ☐ _____
- ☐ _____

ANSWERS

FIND IT IN *THE REALM*: *Story Arc*

Who are the main characters? There are actually two in this story:
1. Graisia
2. Adan

Re-read pages 1 & 2. What is the setting? There are two settings as well: <u>One of the settings is Sawtong, the dump town where Graisia and Adan live. The second setting shown in this section is the world of dreams.</u>

What is Graisia's main external problem or conflict, which is set up in these first two pages? See if you can also find another external as well as an internal problem Graisia has.
<u>Graisia's main external problem is that Adan is after her, and she doesn't know why. Another external problem is basic survival (food, etc). An internal problem is Graisia's fear of Adan. At this point, we don't know what this fear might be keeping her from, but we know she is going to have to deal with it a lot.</u>

Look at page 47 and see if you can figure out what Adan's main problem is.
<u>Adan's main problem is keeping his family's power in the town and making sure someone else does not take his role as Spirit Priest.</u>

FIND IT IN *THE REALM*: *Themes*

Can you think of any other themes in *The Awakening Begins*?
<u>(possible themes:) Graisia finds that life is not about doing, but being. The story teaches about poverty and its affect on lives. Salim and Estar's story lines show that grace and second chances are available.</u>

FIND IT IN *THE REALM*: *More On Characters*

From book 1, what part of Salim's history do you think explains why he is so afraid to try and bring positive changes to Sawtong?
<u>Once, he tried to tell other people about Uri, but for some reason it didn't work. Also, Salim's son, Danjall, rejected following Uri and told everyone not to mention they were related to each other.</u>

Knowing some of Graisia's history, why do you think Graisia is not as rough around the edges or as cruel as Kaly?

Graisia believes that her mother loves her because she can remember her mother crying when she left Graisia. Graisia also hasn't had to live in the city where life can be even harsher than in the slum.

FIND IT IN *THE REALM*: *Senses*

flickered like flames: **sight** and possibly **touch** (heat)
feel his stale: **smell** or **taste**
warm breath: **touch**
full of slithering worms: **touch**
Terror raced up and down her spine like needle pricks, and splinters pressed into her back from the rough wood: **touch**

YOU TRY IT *Dialogue*

Lola and Marcus sat on the front steps of Lola's house.

"What did you do for the summer"? Lola asked.

"Well" Marcus answered "we went to the lake a few times. That was fun," He threw a pebble across the lawn like he was skipping it on the lake, "how about your family?"

Lola smiled, "we went to my grandmother's house."

"That doesn't sound too fun." Marcus responded, "why are you smiling?"

"Oh! My grandmother is a wonderfully entertaining storyteller, my cousins were there, there's an enormous bookstore nearby, the beach isn't far away, and—"

"Okay, okay! I get the picture"! Marcus laughed

"Yeah, it was pretty good" She said as she leaned back on her elbows. "Are you doing anything for Christmas break?

"Christmas?" he was stunned, "we haven't even started school up again!"

"Well what would you want to do?" she loved to think ahead.

Marcus shook his head and smiled, "I'd rather just enjoy your company right now. There's time to think of that later."

FIND IT IN *THE REALM*: *Heads Up on Sequels*

(Spoiler Alert! If you haven't read book 2, you might not want to read the answers below)

Below are some elements from book 2 that were foreshadowed in book 1 – you may have found others as well or instead!

- The Prime Minister, Vivi Sel Luan, is mentioned in book 1 because I knew she would become a more prominent character in book 2.
- There are certain timing issues regarding Adan's mom disappearing and Graisia's age mentioned in book 1 that match with revelations regarding Reyna in book 2.
- Rawiya's prophecy over Soliel in book 1 regarding restoring the old ways speaks of what Soliel will be involved with in book 2 and beyond.
- At the end of book 1, Mahalan threatens Adan saying he isn't finished with Adan, and Adan still belongs to him. This hints at troubles Adan runs into in book 2.

The following are summaries of the new problems and solutions involving Graisia and Adan in book 2. You may have found different ways of saying them.

Graisia: She has multiple problems, both internal and external. The overarching problem she perceives, however, is SAFETY. Whether it's needing to stay safe from Adan, Handro,[9] the nuclear power plant, or in the city, she almost never feels safe. Part of her attempted solution is to follow Soliel and see if what she has is any better than what Salim has taught her. Another solution she tries is going to the city. The ultimate solution she finds is trusting in Uri.

Adan: Adan still wants to rule in Sawtong, but now must choose the best way. Once he chooses to follow Uri and rule with Jarón, his struggle is to learn to rule a different way. He learns that when he is weak, Jarón can actually act more powerfully. Other problems Adan has are safety and gaining Graisia's trust. He finds safety in Uri and eventually proves trustworthy to Graisia.

---

[9] For the first printing of The Awakening Begins, "Handro" was spelled "Jandro." We changed this for future printings so readers wouldn't confuse Jandro and Jarón. Jandro and Handro are pronounced the same, and are the same man.

LINKS

Educational Resources
Downloadable teacher's resources and online student activities
www.TheRealmSeries.com

The Realm Series
Info and a place to sign up to be notified of future releases
www.TheRealmSeries.com

Author Site
Info on speaking engagements and links to
Blog with contests, offers, questions, etc.
www.KLGlanville.com

Publisher
Luminations Media Group Inc.
www.LuminationsMedia.com

Made in the USA
Middletown, DE
21 August 2016